Monkey Series

# True and False Monkey

D1438361

 Foreign Languages Press

First Edition 2007
Second Printing 2010

**True and False Monkey**

ISBN 978-7-119-05065-2


© Foreign Languages Press, China, 2007

*Published by* Foreign Languages Press
24 Baiwanzhuang Road, Beijing 100037, China
Home Page: http://www.flp.com.cn
Email Address: infp@flp.com.cn
             sales@flp.com.cn

Distributed by China International Book Trading Corporation
35 Chegongzhuang Xilu, Beijing 100044, China
P.O. Box 399 Beijing, China

*Printed in the People's Republic of China*

# Monkey Raises Havoc in Jindou Cave

*Monkey Raises Havoc in Jindou Cave*, tells how the Tang Priest, Pig and Friar Sand are caught by the resident demon king when they pass Jindou Cave. Monkey fights the demon to save his master and fellow disciples, but he is foiled by the demon's magic ring. Monkey goes to Heaven to ask the gods to catch the demon, but to their surprise the magic ring works great miracles. Only with the help of the Buddha is the demon, who is actually Lord Lao Zi's water buffalo,finally defeated and the Tang Priest, Pig and Friar Sand saved.

The last story told how the Great King of Miraculous Response of
the River of Heaven made the Tang Priest and his disciples fall
through the ice into the chilly river. Monkey fought the monster
and saved his master. The four then left the River of Heaven and
continued their journey to the West.

One day as the four pilgrims were going over a high mountain, the Tang Priest pointed to a gully and said, "Disciple, look at the towers and houses over there. Let us go and beg some food before we continue on our way." Monkey immediately took a hard look. He saw evil-looking mists and clouds hanging over the place.

Monkey said to the Tang Priest, "Master, that's a bad place." "It may not be a good place, but I'm truly hungry," the Tang Priest responded. Monkey helped the Tang Priest down from his horse and said, "Let me go to beg food for you." He drew a circle on the ground with his gold-banded cudgel and told the three of them to sit inside the circle, warning them over and over not to leave the circle, or terrible things would happen.

Monkey set off due south on his cloud. When he saw a farmhouse amid some ancient trees, he brought his cloud down. An old man was coming out of the house. Monkey went up to him and said politely, "Venerable benefactor, I'm with the monk sent to the Western Heaven by the Great Tang emperor in the East to worship the Buddha and return with the scriptures. My master is hungry; please give him food to eat."

The old man replied immediately, "Monk, you've lost your way. The main trail west is several hundred miles from here." "No, I'm not lost. It took me less time to get there than it would to drink a cup of tea. My master is now sitting by the main trail, waiting for me to bring him some food," said Monkey with a smile.

The old man was alarmed and thought:"This monk's a demon — a demon!" He was just about to go back inside when Monkey took hold of him. The old man lost his temper and raised his stick to hit Monkey. "Hit me as much as you like. I'm keeping score; you'll have to give me a pint of rice for every blow," Monkey said.

The old man rushed inside, shut the door and shouted, "A demon, a demon!" This made the whole household shake with fear. Seeing the door shut, Monkey cast a spell and went straight to the kitchen.

The kitchen smelled of steamed rice. Monkey took the cover off the pot and saw the pot was half full. He thrust his begging bowl into it, filled it to the brim, and went back on his cloud.

Meanwhile, the Tang Priest had been sitting in the circle waiting for Monkey to come back. He looked around and said, "Where has that ape gone to beg for food?" "Goodness knows where he is — probably fooling around," said Pig. "He's left us here in a pen, without shelter from the wind or the cold. It would be better for us to carry on west along the trail."

The Tang Priest thought Pig was right, so, following the idiot's advice, they all left the circle. They soon reached a house with high towers. Pig tethered the horse and let the Tang Priest sit beside the gate out of the wind. Pig shouldered his rake and said, "Let me take a look inside."

Pig went inside and saw three large halls — completely quiet and deserted. There was no furniture in them. When he went around the screen door and farther into the house, he found a big building with half-open upstairs windows through which yellow damask bed-curtains could be seen.

"I suppose they're still in bed because it's so cold," Pig said to himself. He marched up the stairs and was shocked to see a pile of human bones in the bed when he opened the curtain.

When Pig calmed himself, he saw light behind the curtain. He rushed over and found three quilted brocade waistcoats on a coloured lacquer table. He took the three waistcoats out and shouted to his master, "We're really in luck. There's no sign of life there, so I've brought these back with me. It's cold; let's wear them to keep warm."

"No, no," said the Tang Priest. "You'd better take them back." Pig didn't listen and put one on. Friar Sand also tried one. The two were delighted.

As soon as they had tightened the belts they collapsed, unable to stay on their feet. Suddenly the two waistcoats became ropes and tied their hands together. The Tang Priest stamped his feet in indignation. He rushed forward to untie them, but could not.

As they began to despair, the towers and buildings disappeared, and a huge cave rose in front of them. The buildings were just the magic of an evil spirit who had been waiting there to catch people. Now many little demons came rushing out of the cave and took the three of them inside.

The little demons pushed the Tang Priest before the old demon. The Tang Priest pleaded, "Don't be angry, Your Majesty. I have been sent to bring back the scriptures from the Western Heaven. As I was hungry, I sent my senior disciple to beg for food. He has not come back yet, and we blundered into your immortal hall to shelter from the wind. My disciples took your clothes to protect themselves from cold. I shall ask them to return them to you. I beg your mercy; please spare our lives."

"Oh, you're the Tang Priest. I've heard people say that by eating your flesh, the old can become young. You've come without even having been asked, so how can I spare you? What's the name of your senior disciple?" the demon asked with a grin. "My elder brother is Sun Wukong, the Great Sage Equalling Heaven, who created havoc in Heaven five hundred years ago," Pig answered.

This news knocked the demon speechless. "I've long heard of that damned ape's enormous powers." he thought. "We'd better prepare for him." He ordered his demons to tie the three of them and had them carried to the back. The demons sharpened their weapons, ready to attack the Monkey King.

Meanwhile, Monkey had come back with the food. He found the circle he had drawn, but the travellers and horse had disappeared. When he looked where the buildings had been, he saw they had vanished. There were only mountains and grotesquely shaped rocks. "They've been caught," Monkey thought with horror. He rushed after them, following the horse's hoof prints westwards.

While searching, Monkey saw an old man and a boy coming towards him. Monkey went up to the old man and said, "Greetings,
grandfather. Have three monks passed by here?" "They were caught
by the demon king of Jindou Cave. The demon is very powerful.
You'd better run for your life." the old man said.

Monkey replied, "My master is in trouble. I must save him." Thanking the old man, he turned to leave. Suddenly he heard voice behind his back: "Great Sage, we two are the mountain deity and local god waiting here to meet you." Monkey saw them bowing to the ground.

"If you were waiting for me, why did you disguise yourselves?"
Monkey shouted at them. "Because you have such a quick temper,
Great Sage, and we did not want to rush in and offend you," the
local god replied. "That was why we disguised ourselves to tell you
about the demon." Monkey calmed down. He hitched up his tiger-
skin kilt and headed straight for the mountain in search of the cave.

As he rounded some rocks he found a stone cave beside a cliff. Out-side the cave a crowd of little devils were practising with swords and spears. Monkey shouted at the top of his voice, "Little devils, go and tell your master that I'm Sun Wukong, the Great Sage Equal-ling Heaven. Tell him to send my master out at once if the whole lot of you don't want to be killed."

One little devil hurried in to report. "Your Majesty, there's a monk at the gate. He's called Sun Wukong, the Great Sage Equalling Heaven, and he's asking for his master." The demon was delighted to hear this. "Just the person I wanted to see," he said.

All the big and little devils in the cave armed themselves and quickly brought a steel spear to the old demon. They all want out of the cave with the demon.

Outside the cave the demon shouted, "Where is Sun Wukong?"
Monkey stepped forward and answered, "Grandpa Sun is here. Give
me back my master; otherwise there'll be nowhere to bury your
remains." "I'll get you, you impudent devil of an ape!" the demon
roared back. "What powers do you have that give you the nerve to
talk like that?"

Monkey sneered at the demon and shouted, "Shut up, damned beast! Come here and taste my cudgel!" The demon thrust his spear at Monkey. After thirty hard-fought rounds neither of them had won or lost.

The demon king touched the ground with the tip of his spear and ordered his little devils forward. Monkey was completely unafraid. He threw his cudgel into the air and shouted, "Change!" A thousand cudgels rained down from the sky, terrifying the devils out of their wits.

"Behave yourself, ape," said the demon with a mocking laugh, "and watch this trick." He pulled from his sleeve a ring and threw it into the air with a shout of "Get them!" It came whirling down, catching all the cudgels inside it. Monkey somersaulted away to save his life, as he was now disarmed.

"The demon must be an evil star from Heaven," Monkey thought.
"I'd better go up to Heaven to find out." At once he vaulted up on
his cloud, going straight to the Southern Gate of Heaven. He greeted
the four marshals in front of the Hall of Miraculous Mist and told
them he wanted to see the Jade Emperor.

The four marshals reported to the Jade Emperor at once. Having heard Monkey's report, the Jade Emperor straightway sent an order to the star officer to inspect all the stars in the sky and find out if any of them had gone down to earth for love of worldly things.

The Jade Emperor told Monkey to select some heavenly generals to go down to earth with him to catch the demon. Monkey selected the Heavenly King Li the Pagoda Carrier, Prince Nezha and other gods. They were soon at Mount Jindou.

The Heavenly King Li brought his cloud to a stop and asked the Monkey King to send Nezha into battle first. They went straight to the entrance of the cave. "Vicious fiend," shouted Monkey, "open up at once and give me back my master!"

The demon led his little devils out and saw Nezha. "You're Heavenly King Li's third son. Why are you here shouting at my door?"
said the demon with a smile. "Because you have made trouble, vicious fiend, by harming the holy monk from the East. I'm here to
arrest you on the command of the Jade Emperor," Nezha shouted.
The demon roared and pointed his spear at Nezha, who raised his
sword. The battle began.

They fought many rounds without either one being defeated. Nezha used magic to give himself three heads and six arms and hacked at the demon with six weapons. The demon king then gave himself three heads and six arms too, holding spears to protect himself.

Nezha next used his demon-subduing power and threw his six weapons into the air. He shouted "Change!" and each of the six weapons turned into hundreds of such weapons and came flying at the demon.

The demon king was not afraid in the least. Taking out his ring, he threw it into the air with a shout of "Catch them!" It came whistling down and trapped all the weapons. Nezha was terrified and fled for his life empty-handed. The demon king returned to his cave in triumph.

Nezha returned to Heavenly King Li in great anger. "Don't be upset," Monkey said with a laugh. "It is said that fire can damage the ring. Let me go to the Palace of Crimson Splendour and ask the Star Lord of Fire to come here and start a fire to burn the demon." Everyone was very happy to hear this and urged Monkey to return as soon as possible.

Monkey went on his auspicious cloud straight to the Palace of Crimson Splendour. He told the Star Lord of Fire what he had come for. When the Star Lord of Fire heard, he mustered his divine troops and went with Monkey to Mount Jindou.

When the Heavenly King Li saw the Star Lord of Fire, he challenged the demon to battle. The demon led his horde out of the cave. "Vicious monster, send the Tang Priest out at once," Heavenly King Li shouted as he thrust his sword at the demon. The demon dodged the jab and thrust back with his spear.

When the fight was at its fiercest, the demon produced his ring again. When the Heavenly King Li saw this, he fled in defeat. At once the Star Lord of Fire ordered his troops to release all their fire together.

The demon threw his ring into the air, and as it came whistling down it caught the fire dragons and fire horses.

Monkey thought for a while: "If the demon is not afraid of fire, he must be afraid of water. I'm going to ask the Star Lord of Water to flood the cave." He immediately went to the Northern Gate of Heaven. When the Star Lord of Water learned why Mokey had come, he ordered the god of the Yellow River to go with him.

As they arrived at the gate of the cave Monkey shouted, "Open up, devils!" Taking his ring, the demon king was ready to come out again. Just as the doors opened, the river god threw all the water in his white jade bottle into the cave.

Seeing it coming, the demon threw down his spear and quickly took out his ring to seal the inner doors.

The sight filled Monkey with alarm. He charged at the demon king's doors, lashing out with both fists and shouting, "Where do you think you're going? I'll get you!" When he heard this, the demon king came out through the doors, his spear at the ready, and said, "Impudent ape, you've tried and failed to beat me several times. Why are you here again? Why throw your life away?" Monkey said nothing but held up his fists to beat the demon.

Throwing his spear away, the demon took up a fighting stance with both fists raised. The two fought fiercely. Standing to one side, the gods cheered for Monkey, while on the other side the devilish horde all came forward with banners and drums to cheer their master on.

While they were fighting, Monkey pulled out a handful of hairs, scattered them in the air, and with a shout of "Change!" turned them into several dozen little monkeys. They rushed forward, put their arms around the demon's legs and grabbed him by the waist.

The demon, alarmed, pulled out his ring. When Monkey saw the ring, he turned his cloud away and fled back to the top of the mountain. As soon as the demon threw the ring into the air it came whistling down and caught the little monkeys. The demon took them into the cave with his troops.

All the gods suggested that Monkey get the ring by trickery. Monkey thought they had the right idea, so he jumped down from the peak. At the mouth of the cave he turned himself into a fly and crawled through the crack between the doors. He saw the demon sitting on a high throne drinking and eating.

Monkey inched his way towards the throne, but even after taking a long look, he could not find the ring. He quickly flew to the back hall and saw his gold-banded cudgel leaning against the eastern wall. This made him so happy that he turned back to his original form. Picking up the cudgel, he fought his way straight out of the cave.

When the demon heard about this, he led his little devils out. "Where
are you going, damned demon?" Monkey shouted. "Take this!"
Warding off the blow with his spear, the demon insulted Monkey
in reply: "Thieving ape! You're a disgrace. How dare you steal my
property in broad daylight?" "You got my cudgel by using your ring.
How can you say it is yours?" Monkey answered. Once again they
fought each other.

As night was falling, the demon retreated into the cave. Monkey had won the battle. All the gods praised him. "Don't flatter me. The demon must be tired by this fight. I'll go back to the cave, steal the ring, catch the demon, collect your weapons and bring them back to Heaven," Monkey replied.

Arriving at the mouth of the cave, Monkey shook himself and became a spider, squeezing through the crack between the doors.

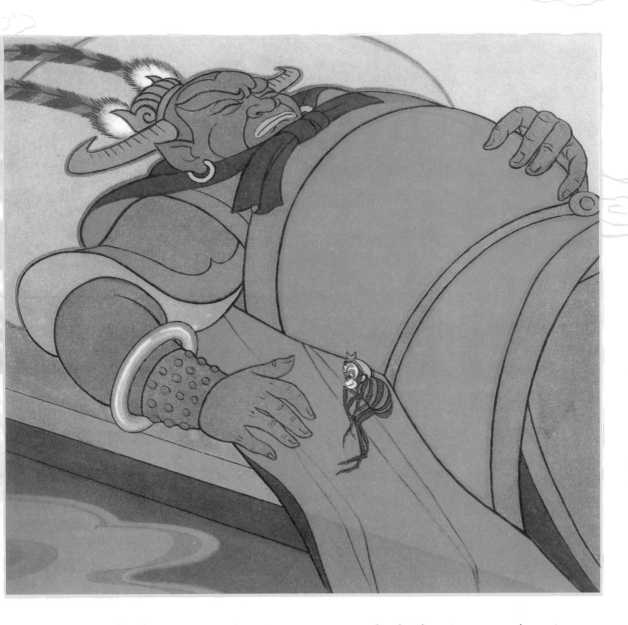

The demon was sleeping on a stone bed. The ring was gleaming on his arm. Monkey changed himself into a flea, jumped onto the bed, and bit the demon so hard that he pushed the ring up even higher on his arm.

Seeing that he couldn't steal the ring for the time being, Monkey jumped down from the bed. Suddenly he heard the groans and whimpers of the fire dragons and fire horses. He turned back to his own form, went to a back door and opened the lock by magic. He noticed inside some of the gods' weapons and a handful of hairs on a table.

Picking up the hairs, Monkey shouted, "Change!" The hairs turned into dozens of little monkeys. He ordered them to take up the weapons, then burn the cave from inside out. All the big and little demons were thrown into panic and ran for their lives.

Monkey rode a fire dragon and led the little monkeys straight up to the peak. Seeing them coming, the gods rushed to get their weapons. Monkey shook himself and put all the hairs back on his body.

It was daylight. Monkey said, "We should fight the demon while his morale is still low. This time I'll be able to catch him." All the gods agreed. "You're right!" Heading for the mouth of the cave, Monkey shouted, "Come out, damned demon!"

The noise caused the monster great alarm. Carrying his spear and his treasure, he rushed out of the cave, cursing.

Monkey thrust at the demon with his cudgel. The demon parried the blow with his spear. All the gods flung their magic weapons at the demon king.

The demon king laughed mockingly, brought forth his ring and threw it into the air. It came whistling down, catching all the weapons of the gods.

Once again the gods were empty-handed. Everybody was unhappy. Trying to look cheerful, Monkey said with a smile, "Don't be upset. Victory and defeat are all part of the soldier's routine. Don't worry. I'll go to the Western Heaven and make some inquiries from the Buddha about who and what he is."

With a shout of "Go!" and one bound of his somersault cloud he
was soon at Vulture Peak. Bringing down his auspicious cloud, he
looked all around. Noble towers and pavilions were shining in the
clouds. Bells and chimes were ringing and voices could be heard
reciting holy sutras. It was a wonderful place.

The Buddha had known Monkey would come. He asked him to come in immediately. Monkey told him what had happened in Jindou Cave and requested the Buddha to find out what sort of creature the demon was. The Buddha opened his all-seeing eyes and discovered the origin of the demon.

Saying nothing to Monkey, the Buddha then told his eighteen arhats to take eighteen grains of golden cinnabar sand with them. Whithout delay the arhats fetched the golden cinnabar sand and set out, while Monkey thanked the Buddha once more. They were soon at Mount Jindou.

Coming out of the cave, the demon shouted, "Thieving ape, you got nothing the last few times. Why are you here again? Soon I'm going to slaughter those three monks. Don't you realize that yet? Get lost!" Hearing this, Monkey could not hold back his anger a moment longer. Raising his cudgel, he hit the demon.

When the arhats saw this, they threw their golden cinnabar sand at the demon all together. The demon was blinded by the flying sand. Alarmed, he threw up his ring once. It caught all eighteen grains of golden cinnabar sand.

Then the arhat Tiger Queller said to Monkey, "The Buddha told us before we left that if we lost the golden cinnabar sand, we should go to Lord Lao Zi at Tushita Palace. He can capture the monster easily." Monkey was very happy. Shouting "I'm off!" he sent his somersault cloud straight through the Southern Gate of Heaven.

Monkey looked around after he got to the Tushita Palace. Suddenly he saw an immortal boy sleeping by the buffalo pen, but the water buffalo was missing. Monkey shouted, "Your buffalo's escaped! Your buffalo's escaped!" Lord Lao Zi was shocked to see this.

Lord Lao Zi woke the boy, then asked, "Has he stolen anything from here? Monkey answered, "He has a ring, a terrible ring."

Carrying his plantain-leaf fan, Lord Lao Zi went on an auspicious cloud with Monkey. When they reached Mount Jindou, Lord Lao Zi asked Monkey to trick the demon and he was going to catch the monster himself. Monkey went to the mouth of the cave and started yelling abuse once more. "Bloated evil beast, come out and be killed!" The demon came out with his spear and his magic ring.

The demon went after Monkey. Suddenly a roar came from the top of the mountain: "Go home, buffalo. What are you here for?" When the demon looked up and saw Lord Lao Zi, he trembled with fear.

Then Lord Lao Zi recited a spell and waved his fan once, and the demon surrendered the ring. Lord Lao Zi grabbed the ring immediately. When he fanned again, the demon changed into a water buffalo.

Riding on the back of the buffalo, Lord Lao Zi said good-bye to Monkey and went straight home to the Tushita Palace.

Monkey and the other heavenly gods charged into the cave, killing all the little devils and recovering their weapons and equipment. Then all the gods said good-bye to Monkey and went back to Heaven.

Finally, Monkey released the Tang Priest, Pig and Friar Sand. The four of them packed their baggage and left the cave to find the main route to the West.

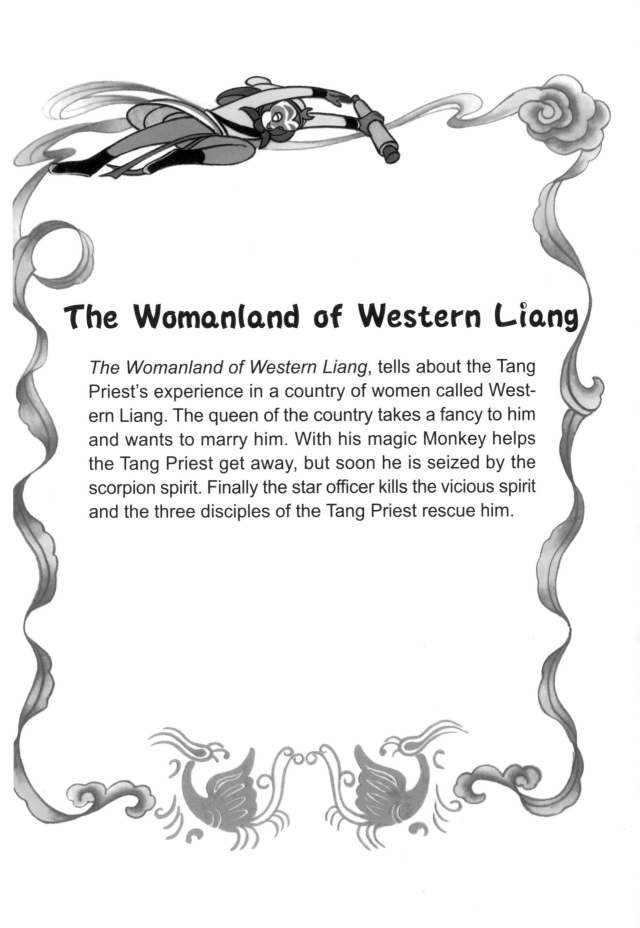

# The Womanland of Western Liang

*The Womanland of Western Liang*, tells about the Tang Priest's experience in a country of women called Western Liang. The queen of the country takes a fancy to him and wants to marry him. With his magic Monkey helps the Tang Priest get away, but soon he is seized by the scorpion spirit. Finally the star officer kills the vicious spirit and the three disciples of the Tang Priest rescue him.

After the Tang Priest and his disciples had left the cave and gone about a dozen miles, they saw a city. The Tang Priest said, "That must be the capital of the Womanland of Western Liang. You must behave yourselves and not betray the teachings of our Buddhist faith."

Before the Tang Priest had finished speaking, they reached the east gate of the city. All the people, old and young, were women, with skirts and jackets and powdered faces.

As soon as the people on the street caught sight of the four men, they clapped, laughed and shouted, "Men are coming! Men are coming!" The four could not move forward.

So Pig made a hideous face clear the way. He shook his head, pointed his ears, twisted his snout and gave a roar that frightened all the women away.

Then master and disciples continued on their way. Suddenly an official standing in the street shouted to them, "Envoys from afar, you may not enter the city gates without permission. Please go to the reception centre for men and register."

Hearing this, the Tang Priest dismounted and greeted the official. She led them into the main hall of the reception centre and asked them where they were from and what business had brought them there. Then she said, "I am only the superintendent of the reception centre for men. Please make yourselves comfortable while I go to report to our queen." The Tang Priest said, "Please go ahead!"

The superintendent went straight into the city and reported to the queen, "The Tang Priest, the younger brother of the Tang Emperor in the East, with his three disciples is passing through our country on his way to the West to fetch the Buddhist scriptures. I have come especially to ask Your Majesty' s approval of their passage."

The queen was delighted to hear this and said, "We have never seen a man in our country under all the queens who have reigned here. The fortunate arrival of the Tang emperor's younger brother must be a gift from Heaven. I should like to persuade him to become my king, then we can produce sons and grandsons to inherit the throne."

All the officials rejoiced, then one of them said, "Your Majesty, we have no matchmaker to arrange the marriage." So the queen chose the royal tutor as matchmaker and the superintendent of the reception centre as the mistress of ceremonies. Then they went to the reception centre to get the consent of the emperor's younger brother.

The two officials entered, bowed low before the Tang Priest and said, "Congratulations!" The Tang Priest did not understand. "I am a monk. What good fortune are you congratulating me for?" The tutor told him about the queen's proposal. As soon as the Tang Priest heard, he waved his hand and said, "No, no!"

Pig, standing beside them, pointed to himself and said, "My master is very anxious to get to the West to bring back the Buddhist scriptures. You can keep me here instead to be her husband." The tutor was shocked by Pig's ugly appearance and remained speechless. "Idiot, stop that nonsense!" said Monkey.

The Tang Priest grabbed Monkey and asked, "What are we going to do?" Monkey replied, "Don't worry. Let me deal with this."

Monkey turned to the tutor and said, "What the royal tutor says is right. We'll let our master stay here as the queen's husband. Quickly give us back our travel documents so the three of us can go on our way west."

Then Pig said, "Tutor, now we've agreed, get your mistress to lay on a banquet so that we can all drink a cup of engagement wine." "Yes, yes," said the tutor and the superintendent, "a banquet will be provided." Then they went in great delight to report back to the queen.

The Tang Priest cursed Monkey. "How could you say such a thing! Making me stay here to be her husband while you go to the Western Heaven to worship the Buddha! I'd die before I agreed to do that." "Don't worry, Master," said Monkey. "If you had refused her, she would not have returned our travel paper or let us continue on our way."

The Tang Priest said, "I'm afraid that the queen will want me to perform husbandly duties against the Buddhist creed." Monkey whispered to the Tang Priest, and he nodded his head to show his satisfaction.

The tutor and superintendent reported to the queen, "Your Majesty's dream has come true. The only thing is that his three disciples want an engagement feast first." When the queen heard this, she ordered her officers to lay on a banquet and she had the state carriage prepared to take her to welcome her lord.

Soon the queen arrived at the reception centre. The Tang Priest and his disciples went to meet her. "Dear emperor's brother, won't you get into my dragon and phoenix coach and ride back with me to the throne hall," she said affectionately. This made the Tang Priest blush from ear to ear. He was too embarrassed to look at her.

Then the queen and the Tang Priest entered the royal coach, sitting side by side. The three disciples followed the coach with their baggage and horse.

Descending from the coach hand in hand, the queen and the Tang Priest went into the palace. A banquet was set out in the eastern hall.

The queen proposed repeated toasts to the Tang Priest. Pig did not worry about anything as he relaxed his belly and ate for all he was worth.

At the end of the banquet the Tang Priest bowed to the queen and said, "Your Majesty, I am very grateful for this sumptuous banquet. We have had enough now. Could you go to the throne hall and return the passport so my disciples can be sent on their way?"

The queen sent for a brush, ink stone and the imperial jade seal. She stamped the passport with her royal seal and signed her name. Then an official gave it to Friar Sand.

"May I have Your Majesty's permission to escort my disciples out of the city?" the Tang Priest asked. The queen nodded approval, sent for her coach and they rode westwards out of the city.

Everyone poured into the streets with fine incense and drums to see the queen in her carriage and the emperor's younger brother.

When they were outside the western gate the Tang Priest stepped down from the royal carriage, bowed to the queen and said, "Please go back now, Your Majesty, and allow me to go on to fetch the scriptures." The queen was shocked. She grabbed the Tang Priest and said, "How can you go back on your word?"

Pig rushed to the royal coach, thrusting his snout about and waving his huge ears. The queen was so frightened she collapsed in the coach.

When the tutor saw what was happening, she gave an order, and eight soldiers rushed forward and pushed Pig away. Then they tried to take the Tang Priest away.

Monkey thought he'd better use his magic to stop all the women; otherwise they would never get away.

Just at that moment a woman rushed from the roadside, shouting, "Don't go, Tang emperor's brother. You and I are going to be husband and wife."

Friar Sand struck at her head with his staff. The woman then created a whirlwind that carried the Tang Priest off with a great roar.

The three disciples hastily sprang into the air to catch the whirlwind.

They chased it to a high mountain, where the wind stopped and the grey dust settled, so they did not know which way the Tang Priest had gone.

The brothers brought their clouds down to land to search all around. Suddenly behind a gleaming rock they noticed two stone doors; carved above them was DEADLY FOE MOUNTAIN PIPA CAVE. Pig went up to the doors and was about to beat on them with his rake.

Monkey rushed forward to stop him. "Don't be in such a hurry," he said. "I'm going to take a look around and find out what's happening here." Then he turned into an exquisite bee and squeezed through the crack between the outer doors.

He flew past the inner doors and saw a female monster, simple and charming, dressed in bright-coloured clothes, sitting in a flower pavilion. The Tang Priest was standing there, trembling with fear.

The female monster was talking to the Tang Priest. "Don't worry, Emperor's Brother. It may not be so rich and splendid here as the palace in the Womanland of Western Liang, but it's peaceful and comfortable. With me as your companion you'll be able to live in harmony."

Monkey resumed his own appearance and shouted, "Behave yourself, you evil beast!" Then the monster seized her steel trident and leapt through the door of the pavilion, shouting abusively, "Hooligan ape! How dare you sneak into my house to set your dirty eyes on me. Stay where you are and take this!"

Monkey parried the lunge from her trident and fell back, fighting all the way. When they reached the outside of the cave, Pig joined the fighting, raising his rake with both hands and rushing forward.

Suddenly the monster breathed smoke out of her nose and fire from her mouth as she jabbed Monkey's head with her trident. Monkey yelled in agony at the unbearable pain and fled.

The monster put her steel trident away and went back. Monkey held his head and shouted, "It's terrible, it's terrible!"

The three disciples were at a loss as to what to do when they noticed an old woman with a bamboo basket full of wild vegetables. "Brother," said Friar Sand to Monkey, "I'll ask that woman who this evil spirit is."

Taking a quick look Monkey recognized that it was none other than the Bodhisattva Guanyin. Monkey immediately fell to his knees and said, "Bodhisattva, please forgive your disciple for failing to come to meet you. We are now up against a monster we can't beat and we beseech you, Bodhisattva, to help us."

The Bodhisattva changed to her true form and replied, "She is indeed a very terrible monster. She was originally a scorpion spirit. If you want to overcome her, go to the Palace of Light inside the Eastern Gate of Heaven and look for the Star Officer of the Pleiades."

Then she turned into a beam of golden light and went straight back to the Southern Sea.

Monkey set off at once on his cloud and was outside the Eastern Gate of Heaven in an instant.

When Monkey saw the Star Officer of the Pleiades, he explained to him what had happened and said, "I have come especially to beg you to rescue my master."

The Star Officer of the Pleiades left the Palace of Light at once and went straight to Deadly Foe Mountain with Monkey.

When they arrived at the Pipa Cave, Pig and Friar Sand greeted them.
Pig said wrathfully, "Let's go and fight that vicious creature."

Pig smashed the doors of the cave with his rake. The monster, with fierce, round eyes, leapt out of the cave and thrust her trident at Pig.

The Star Officer stood on the mountainside, changing into a giant rooster. When he crowed, the monster collapsed to the ground and her face turned white.

When the rooster crowed again, the monster reverted to her true appearance as a scorpion spirit. Pig pounded her to mincemeat with his rake.

The Star Officer turned back into his original form and rode away on his cloud. Monkey, Pig and Friar Sand all clasped their hands in thanks.

The three of them went into the cave and found their master sitting in a room at the back. They helped the Tang Priest back on the horse, then lit a firebrand and burned down all the buildings in the cave. Then the four pilgrims continued on their way to the West. If you want to know what happened to them next, read the next story.

# True and False Monkey

*True and False Monkey*, tells this story: After a fight with bandits who tried to rob the Tang Priest, Monkey discovers another Monkey who looks just like him. When the two meet, they fight endlessly as they go to the Bodhisattva Guanyin, the Jade Emperor, the Tang Priest and the Lords of the Underworld to be told apart, but no one can tell the true Monkey from the false one. Finally the two Monkeys go to Sakyamuni Buddha, who shows everyone the false Monkey is really a six-eared macaque.

The last instalment told how Monkey rescued the Tang Priest from the Pipa Cave, and master and disciples continued on their journey to the West. One day a high mountain rose up in front of them and the Tang Priest called out, "Be careful, Monkey, I'm afraid there may be demons on that steep mountain." "Don't worry, Master," Monkey said. "You needn't be scared of demons while I'm here." The Tang Priest was happy to hear this.

When the four of them went down the western slopes of the mountain and came on a stretch of level ground, it was getting late. Monkey shouted to the horse to go faster. The horse shot ahead like an arrow and didn't slow down until it had covered six or seven miles.

As the Tang Priest was riding along he heard a gong being struck, and over thirty bandits emerged from both sides of the road to block his way. "Don't go any farther, monk," the two burly fellows heading the gang shouted. "Give us your money, or we'll kill you!" Much frightened, the Tang Priest fell off his horse, pleading loudly, "Spare my life, Your Majesties! Spare my life, Your Majesties!"

Just at this moment Monkey arrived. He swung his cudgel and struck and killed the two bandit chiefs, sending the others fleeing for their lives. The venerable monk could not stand such a bloody scene. He told Pig to bury the dead, then he scattered earth on the grave, burned incense and began to pray. After this he scolded Monkey for having killed the living.

The four set out again for the West. When they came to a farmhouse, the Tang Priest knocked at the gate. An old man came out. The Tang Priest, greeting him, said, "This humble monk has been sent by the Great Tang in the East to fetch the scriptures from the Western Heaven. As it's getting dark, I've come to beg a night's lodging from you."

The old man invited the four into the thatched cottage and told his wife to fetch cups of tea and prepare food. After supper the old man led them to the back room, where they could spend the night.

The old man's son happened to be one of the bandits whose chiefs had been slain by Monkey. Late that night, when he led a group of the robbers back to his home, he was told that the Tang Priest and his disciples were sleeping there. "What luck!" he shouted, ready to avenge his chiefs by murdering the four.

The old man, terrified, hurried stealthily to the back room and opened the back gate to let the Tang Priest and his disciples escape. They had fled just a short distance when they saw the bandits were after them, cursing and waving their weapons. Monkey swung his cudgel and turned to face them. "Monkey," the Tang Priest warned hurriedly, "you are not to hurt them. Just scare them off."

However, Monkey killed all the bandits, including the old man's son. The sight frightened the Tang Priest so much that he rolled off his horse.

The Tang Priest said angrily to Monkey, "Yesterday after you killed the two bandit chiefs, I scolded you for your cruelty, and today you've murdered several more! Don't forget that last night the old gentleman gave us a meal and a night's lodging and opened the back gate to let us escape. Even if his son was a bandit, you shouldn't have killed him. You're too much of a murderer to fetch scriptures. Go at once!" Terrified, Monkey fell on his knees.

Monkey said, "I've got places to go, Master, but I'm afraid you will never reach the Western Heaven without me." Without replying, the Tang Priest began to recite the Band-tightening Spell. Monkey's head was squeezed so tight that his face and ears turned bright red, his eyes bulged and his brain ached.

In unbearable pain and seeing that the master would not change his mind, Monkey had no choice but to go. He shot into the air on his somersault cloud, thinking: "The master has let me down. I'm off to the Southern Sea to make a complaint before the Bodhisattva Guanyin."

On seeing the Bodhisattva, Monkey kowtowed and told her all the details of how the Tang Priest had sent him away because he had killed the bandits. He went on to beg the Bodhisattva to take the Band-tightening Spell off his head and let him go back to live in the Water Curtain Cave. But the Bodhisattva said, "You'd better stay here, for your master will soon come to look for you; he is just about to be wounded."

The Tang Priest was hungry and thirsty after driving Monkey away. He sent Pig to beg for some food and fetch some water, but after a long time there was still no sign of Pig. Tying the horse to a tree, Friar Sand said, "Master, take a good rest. I'm going to fetch some water for you."

While the Tang Priest was enduring his burning thirst, a noise made him open his eyes and look. It was Monkey kneeling before him, holding a pottery cup. "Master," he said, "without me you can't even have water to drink. Please drink this lovely cold water while I go to beg some food for you." "I'd rather die of thirst than drink water you give me. Go away, you wicked ape!"

At that, Monkey turned angry and, shouting "You cruel old baldy!" swung his cudgel, knocking the Tang Priest senseless. Then he picked up their baggage and disappeared on a cloud.

Pig had begged a bowl of leftover rice and was on his way back when he met Friar Sand looking for him. Pig had Friar Sand carry the rice in the fold of his habit so he could fetch water in the bowl, then they cheerfully went back.

But what did they find but the Tang Priest lying unconscious on the ground, no trace of the baggage, and the white dragon horse running to and fro, whinnying. Pig howled in horror, "This must have been done by the survivors of the gang Monkey drove away; they came back, killed Master and took away the baggage. Wait till I sell the horse for a few ounces of silver to buy a coffin to bury Master in, then we can split up and go our separate ways." But Friar Sand would not hear of this. He propped the master up and moaned, "Poor, poor Master!"

The Tang Priest gradually came to. He told the two disciples how Monkey had tried to kill him and stolen the baggage. Pig was furious. "I'm going to find that monkey and get back our bundles." Friar Sand said, "Let's first help Master get to some cottage in the hollow and ask for hot tea to make him better, then we can go to find Monkey."

The three of them begged for some hot tea to drink. When the Tang Priest grew calm again, he said to Pig, "You have never got on with that monkey. Let Friar Sand fetch the baggage." Then he turned to Friar Sand. "If that ape won't give you the bundles, you mustn't quarrel with him. Just go to the Bodhisattva and ask her to demand them from him." Friar Sand nodded and took off on a lightning cloud.

On reaching the Mountain of Flowers and Fruit, Friar Sand landed his cloud and found his way to the Water Curtain Cave. As he approached, he saw the mountain was covered with yelling monkey spirits.

Closer still, he saw Monkey sitting on a stone terrace, holding in both hands the passport given to the Tang Priest by the Emperor of the Great Tang and reading it aloud.

Friar Sand could not help calling out, "Elder Brother, how come you're reading Master's passport out loud?" Monkey shouted back, "Who are you? What a nerve you have coming so near our immortals' cave!" Seeing that Monkey refused to recognize him, Friar Sand went up to him with a bow and said, "If you still remember what you owe our master for delivering you from your torment in the past, bring the baggage and go back with me to see him; if not, please give me the bundles."

Monkey laughed and replied, "The reason I hit the Tang Priest and took the baggage is that I've made up my mind not to follow him anymore to the West; instead I'll go to the Western Heaven to worship the Buddha and fetch the scriptures myself. After taking them back to the East, I'll make people there worship me as a great sage and I'll be famous forever." "What you say isn't right," retorted Friar Sand. "No Lord Buddha is going to give you the scriptures if you turn up without the Tang Priest."

"Brother," said Monkey, "I've chosen another holy monk to escort. Tomorrow we're setting out on our journey." No sooner had he finished than some little monkeys came out leading a white dragon horse, a Tang Priest, a Pig and a Friar Sand carrying the baggage on his monastic staff.

At this Friar Sand in a fury raised his demon-quelling staff with both arms and brought it down on his double's head, killing him outright. It turned out to be a small monkey spirit.

Monkey was so angry that he had all the monkeys surround Friar Sand. Lashing about, Friar Sand fought his way out and escaped by cloud, heading for the Southern Sea to find the Bodhisattva Guanyin.

After reaching Mount Potaraka in the Southern Sea, Friar Sand knelt down before the Bodhisattva. Just as he was about to make his complaint, he spotted Monkey standing beside her. Furious, he struck at Monkey's face with his staff, cursing, "You thoroughly evil, treacherous ape! Now you are trying to deceive the Bodhisattva too."

Instead of hitting back, Monkey dodged the blow. "Don't hit him, Friar Sand," said the Bodhisattva. "Tell me what's happened." Friar Sand gave her all the details. After listening to him, the Bodhisattva laughed and said, "Monkey has been here four days. How could he be in the Water Curtain Cave?"

"But I'm telling you the truth," Friar Sand replied. "Calm down," said the Bodhisattva. "I'll send Monkey back to the Mountain of Flowers and Fruit with you to take a good look round. You can then tell the true from the false." At this Monkey and Friar Sand went straight back to the Mountain of Flowers and Fruit by two beams of auspicious light.

Soon the two were in sight of the Mountain of Flowers and Fruit. They brought down their clouds and took a good look. There was indeed a Monkey sitting on a high stone terrace, drinking and making merry with the other monkeys.

After returning from the Mountain of Flowers and Fruit, Friar Sand told the Tang Priest what had happened. The Tang Priest was very surprised and regretful. "When I said that Monkey had hit me and taken the baggage, I didn't realize that it was an evil spirit that had turned itself into another Monkey." Pig meanwhile roared with laughter.

Friar Sand stood beside them, swinging his staff and longing to join in, but since he could not tell true from the false, he was afraid of wounding the real Monkey. So he shot back down to the cliff, where he fought his way into the Water Curtain Cave to look for the passport and the bundles, but he failed to find them.

He took his cloud back up and swung his staff again, but he was still unable to strike. "Friar Sand," said Monkey, "go back and tell the master what's been happening here while I drive this demon to the Southern Sea so the Bodhisattva can identify me as the real Monkey." The other Monkey repeated what he said.

As the two Monkeys looked and sounded exactly alike, Friar Sand really could not tell them apart, so he turned his cloud to rejoin the Tang Priest.

The two Monkeys fought and shouted their way to the Southern Sea. Their constant shouting disturbed all the divine beings who protected the law, so they hurried to report it to the Bodhisattva Guanyin.

The Bodhisattva shouted, "Stay where you are, evil beast!" At that each Monkey grabbed hold of the other while the real one said, "I'm the real Monkey." The other Monkey retorted, "He's the fake one."

The Bodhisattva then quietly recited the Band-tightening Spell. Both Monkeys cried out in pain, clutched their heads and rolled on the ground, shouting, "Stop, stop!" But the moment she stopped, they grabbed each other again and resumed fighting and shouting.

At her wits' end the Bodhisattva said, "Monkey, you were once appointed Protector of the Horses. When you made havoc in the Heavenly Palace, all the heavenly generals recognized you, so you'd better go to the Heavenly Palace and let them tell you apart." Pulling and tugging at each other, they went straight to the Heavenly Palace.

The two Monkeys fought their way to the Southern Gate of Heaven, where all the gate gods, big and small, blocked the entrance with their weapons and shouted, "Where are you going? This is no place for a brawl." The two told exactly the same story, and no matter how closely the gods looked, they could not tell them apart.

"If you can't tell which is which," the two shouted, "get out of the way and let us go to see the Jade Emperor!" As the gods could not stop them, they let the fighting Monkeys into the Hall of Miraculous Mist.

On seeing the two rush in, the Jade Emperor got so alarmed that he could not speak for a while. The two Monkeys told the same story all over again and asked the Jade Emperor to tell them apart.

The Jade Emperor ordered heavenly King Li the Pagoda Carrier to look at them both in his demon-revealing mirror. The Heavenly King took out his mirror and looked at their reflections; they both looked exactly the same, dressed exactly alike.

So even the Jade Emperor and Heavenly King Li could not tell the true from the false. The two Monkeys then said, "Let's go see Master." Fighting each other on the way out of the Southern Gate of Heaven, the two landed on the road leading westward.

In a burst of rage the real Monkey went up to the false one to strike him with his cudgel. Without a word the fake Monkey went at him with his own iron cudgel. When the two Monkeys were fighting together, there was no way of telling them apart.

As they were talking, they heard a noisy quarrel in midair. The Tang Priest looked up and saw two Monkeys fighting. Itching for a fight, Pig said, "I'm going up to have a look."

With that Pig leapt up into the air and shouted, "Stop yelling, Brother; Pig's here!" "Hit the evil spirit!" both Monkeys said at the same time. "Hit the evil spirit!"

Friar Sand said, "Master, Pig and I will each bring one of them back here, and then you just say the spell. The one who suffers will be the real Monkey." "A good idea," said the Tang Priest.

"Stop fighting!" Friar Sand called. "Go to Master and let him tell you apart." Friar Sand and Pig, each dragging one of the Monkeys, landed their clouds in front of the Tang Priest.

Silently the Tang Priest recited the Band-tightening Spell. "Stop! Stop!" Both Monkeys were suffering. "Why do you have to say that spell when we're fighting so hard?" Being a kind person, the Tang Priest stopped, unable to tell who was who.

The two Monkeys began fighting again. "Brothers," said one, "look after our master while I take him down to ask the Lords of the Underworld to judge." The other Monkey said the same thing. Grabbing and tugging at each other, the two soon disappeared.

Pig asked Friar Sand, "Why didn't you get the passport back when you were in the Water Curtain Cave?" Friar Sand answered, "After I took care of the little monkeys, I looked all over for the passport and bundles, but I couldn't find them."

The Tang Priest said, "Pig, you go to the Mountain of Flowers and Fruit and fetch our baggage while the demon is away. We'll continue our journey to the West. Even if Monkey does come back, I won't have him." "I'm off, then," said Pig. He leapt into the air and headed off by cloud to the Mountain of Flowers and Fruit.

The two Monkeys fought their way to the back of the Dark Mountain of the Underworld, where all the demons shivered with terror as they hid themselves. The first ones to run away rushed to report to the Senluo Palace.

In an instant the Lords of the Underworld gathered their forces.
Soon they heard the roaring of a mighty wind, and fog filled the air.
The two Monkeys came tumbling and rolling into the Senluo Palace.

The Lords of the Underworld stepped forward to block their way and asked, "Great Sages, why are you creating such disorder?" The two Monkeys told the same story one after the other. Upon hearing it, the Lords called on the judge to go through the registers of births and deaths.

The judge reported back that in the monkey section of the registers there was a record of how the Great Sage had raised havoc in the Underworld and removed his name from the registers. At this the Lords of the Underworld said to the Monkeys, "Great Sages, your names are not in the records and so cannot be checked. You'll have to go back to the world of the living to be told apart."

"Wait!" the Bodhisattva King Ksitigarbha shouted. "I'll ask Examiner to tell you apart." Examiner was an animal that could tell good from evil by lying on the ground and listening. It lay down on the ground as it was told to do and listened attentively.

A little later it raised its head and said to Ksitigarbha, "I've found the name of the demon, but I can't say it to his face. The evil spirit's magic powers are as strong as Monkey's, so we can't catch him in the Underworld." "Then how can we get rid of the evil spirit?" "The Buddha's power is boundless," Examiner replied.

Enlightened, Ksitigarbha said, "As you two look the same and have the same magic powers, you will have to go to Sakyamuni Buddha to be told apart." "You're right," the two Monkeys replied together.

They left the Senluo Palace. Grabbing and snatching at each other, they fought and shouted their way to the Thunder Monastery in the Western Heaven.

Sakyamuni Buddha could tell the two apart, but just as he was about to reveal the false Monkey, the Bodhisattva Guanyin arrived. The Buddha told Guanyin, "I can see that the false Monkey is really a six-eared macaque that knows what's happening hundreds of miles away and hears everything that's said. Because it is such an all-powerful creature it can look and sound just like Monkey."

As soon as the macaque heard the Buddha say what it really was, it started shaking with fear and took a great leap to escape, but it was immediately surrouded by the Buddha's warrior attendants.

Seeing this, the macaque's fur stood on end. It shook itself, turned into a bee, and started to fly straight up, only to fall down again as the Buddha's golden begging bowl was clapped over it.

Everyone thought it had fled, but the Buddha said, "The evil spirit is under my bowl." When the bowl was lifted, it appeared in its true form: a six-eared macaque.

Monkey swung his iron cudgel and killed the macaque with a single blow to the head. It was more than the Buddha could bear. "Terrible," he said. "This is terrible."

The Buddha then told Monkey to go back at once to escort the Tang Priest to fetch the scriptures. Monkey kowtowed but said to him, "My master has definitely refused to have me. I beg you in your kindness to say the Band-loosening Spell so that I can take off my gold band and return to ordinary life." "Stop that silly talk," said the Buddha. "I shall ask Guanyin to take you back to your master. Of course he'll accept you."

When the Bodhisattva Guanyin heard this, she put her hands together to thank the Buddha for his mercy, then she took Monkey
away from the Thunder Monastery and together they went by cloud
to find the Tang Priest.

They soon found the Tang Priest and Friar Sand. The Bodhisattva told them about how the Buddha had told the two Monkeys apart and how the six-eared macaque had been killed by Monkey. "Tang Priest," she said, "since there are many demon obstacles on the way ahead, you must take Monkey back and have his protection." The Tang Priest respectfully obeyed.

Just at this moment Pig returned by cloud, carrying the bundles and the passport, which he had found in the Mountain of Flowers and Fruit.

Seeing the Bodhisattva, Pig kowtowed. "Your disciple left the other day for the Water Curtain Cave on the Mountain of Flowers and Fruit to look for the baggage, which I found inside the cave. I've checked it over — nothing's missing. Then I came straight back by cloud."

He asked about the two Monkeys. When he heard that the Buddha had told them apart, Pig was delighted and gave thanks over and over again.

The Tang Priest and his three disciples said farewell to the
Bodhisattva, repacked their baggage and set out again for the West.
They were once again of a single will and a single mind.

■图书在版编目（CIP）数据

真假孙悟空（美猴王丛书）／许力等改编；于长海等绘画／北京：外文出版社，2007.10

■SBN　978-7-119-05065-2

I．真…　II.①许…　②于…　III.故事－作品集－中国－当代－英文　IV.I 247.8

中国版本图书馆 CIP 数据核字（2007）第 121910 号


改　　编：许　力　方　原　高明友
绘　　画：于长海　蔡　荣　胡立滨
特约编辑：李树芬
装帧设计：浩涛工作室
责任编辑：兰佩瑾　蔡跃蕾

**真假孙悟空**

外文出版社出版
（中国北京百万庄大街 24 号）
邮政编码：100037
外文出版社网页：http://www.flp.com.cn
外文出版社电子邮件地址：info@flp.com.cn
　　　　　　　　　　　sales@flp.com.cn
北京外文印刷厂印刷
中国国际图书贸易总公司发行
（中国北京车公庄西路 35 号）
北京邮政信箱第 399 号　邮政编码 100044
2008 年(16 开)第 1 版
2010 年 4 月第 1 版第 2 次印刷
（英文）
ISBN 978-7-119-05065-2
09400
88-E-525P

《美猴王丛书》调整再版，请失去联系的作者与我社联系，我社将按国家标准支付相应报酬。